Welcome to a
World Full of Colours!

Welcome, young explorer! Are you ready to dive into the beautiful and bright world of colours? This book is your guide to understanding all the colours that you see around you every day. From the deep blue of the ocean to the fiery red of a sunset, colours make our world an exciting and wonderful place.

By

Scott Benjamin Gracie

In Lumine Stellas

A catalogue record for this book is available from the National Library of Australia

ISBN   978 0 6456241 4 4 (Hardcover)
ISBN   978 0 6456241 5 1 (eBook)
www.lightdarkeverything.com.au/our-wonderful-world-of-colours

Welcome to a World Full of Colours!

Welcome, young explorer! Are you ready to dive into the beautiful and bright world of colours? This book is your guide to understanding all the colours that you see around you every day. From the deep blue of the ocean to the fiery red of a sunset, colours make our world an exciting and wonderful place.

The Magic of
Light and Colours

Did you know that light is the secret behind all the colours you see? Light may look white, but it's actually made up of many different colours! These colours can be seen when light passes through something like a raindrop or a prism, splitting into a beautiful rainbow.

What is Colour?

Colour is all around us. Coloured light reflects off objects and enters our eyes, helping us see and enjoy the world. Imagine a world without colour – it would be like a garden without flowers or a night sky without stars. But don't worry, our world is full of colours, and you're about to discover how they work and why they are so important!

A Rainbow of Colours

When light splits like this, we can see all the colours of the rainbow. Each colour has its own wavelength, which is why they look different. Red has the longest wavelength, and violet has the shortest. Together, these colours make the world look bright and cheerful. So, the next time you see a rainbow, remember, it's light playing its magical colour game!

The Colour Wheel – A Rainbow in a Circle!

Welcome to the fascinating world of the colour wheel! It's like a rainbow shaped into a circle. The colour wheel helps artists and designers understand how colours work together. It's also a great way for you to learn about different colours and how they mix.

Mixing Colours of Paint or Light

Primary Colours – The Building Blocks

Secondary Colours – Mixing Magic

Tertiary Colours – A Colourful Blend

Mixing paint colours is called subtractive colour mixing.

Mixing coloured light is called additive colour mixing.

Warm Colours – The Colours of Sunshine and Fire

Warm colours are like the colours of the sun and fire – red, orange, and yellow. These colours can make you feel cozy, excited, or happy. They remind us of things like warm sunny days, tasty fruits, and beautiful autumn leaves.

Cool Colours – The Colours of the Ocean and the Sky

Now let's talk about cool colours: green, blue, and purple. These colours can make you feel calm and relaxed. They remind us of things like the peaceful ocean, the vast sky, and lovely flowers.

Colours in Animals – The Art of Camouflage

In nature, animals use colours in amazing ways. One of the most fascinating uses is camouflage. Some animals can change their colour to blend in with their surroundings. Like a chameleon, they can look almost invisible!

Colours in Plants - A Seasonal Symphony

Have you ever wondered why leaves change colour in autumn? It's because of a magical process in nature. In the fall/ Autumn, trees start to prepare for winter. The green colour fades away, and brilliant reds, oranges, and yellows take its place.

Eating a Rainbow

Eating a variety of colours is not only fun but also healthy! Different coloured fruits and vegetables contain different vitamins and nutrients. So, when you eat a rainbow of foods, you're giving your body all the good stuff it needs to grow strong and healthy.

Colours in Art

Artists love using colours to express their feelings and ideas. From bright and happy paintings to calm and soothing drawings, colours play a big part in making art beautiful and meaningful. Just like a painter, you can use colours to show the world how you feel.

Colours and Cultures

Did you know that colours can mean different things in different cultures? For example, red can mean luck and happiness in some cultures, while it can represent warning or danger in others. Colours are a beautiful part of our world's diverse cultures and traditions.

Light and Colours

Colours are a magical part of light. When sunlight passes through a prism or a raindrop, it splits into all the colours we can see. Each colour in the rainbow is a part of the white light. It's like a hidden treasure in sunlight!

Colour Blindness

Not everyone sees colours the same way. Some people have colour blindness, which means they see colours differently. It's not that they only see in black and white, but they might have trouble telling certain colours apart. Understanding colour blindness helps us appreciate the unique ways we all see the world.

Optical Illusions with Colour

Colours can play tricks on our eyes! Optical illusions use colours and shapes to create images that can look different from what they really are. These illusions are fun puzzles for our eyes and brain, showing us how amazing and tricky colours can be.

The Magic of Colour Perception

Our eyes and brain work together to see colours. The way we perceive colours can be affected by lighting, background colours, and even our own feelings. It's a fascinating part of how we experience the world around us, filled with colours and wonders.

Mixing Colours - Discovering New Shades

Mixing colours is like a magical experiment! When you mix primary paint colours - red, yellow, and blue - you can create so many new colours. Red and yellow make orange, yellow and blue make green, and blue and red make purple. It's amazing how just three colours can make so many others!

Colour by Numbers – Artistic Fun

Colour by numbers is a fun way to create beautiful pictures. Each number corresponds to a colour, and by filling in the spaces, a colourful image emerges. It's like solving a colourful puzzle that turns into a piece of art!

Learning Colours Through Play

Playing with colours is not only fun but also a great way to learn. Games like matching colourful shapes and patterns help you recognize and remember different colours and shades. Plus, it's a super enjoyable way to spend your time!

Crafting with Colours

Crafting is another fantastic way to have fun with colours. Using coloured paper, glue, and scissors, you can create colourful collages, decorations, and art. It's a playful way to explore your creativity and see how colours combine to make beautiful creations.

How Colours Affect Mood

Colours can influence how we feel. Warm colours like red and yellow can make us feel happy and energetic, while cool colours like blue and green can make us feel calm and relaxed. It's fascinating how just looking at different colours can change our mood!

Everyone Has a Favorite Colour

Do you have a favourite colour? Most people do! Our favourite colours can say a lot about us. Some people love blue because it reminds them of the sky, others love green because it makes them think of nature. What's your favourite colour and why?

Symbolic Meanings of Colours

Colours can also have meanings. For example, red can symbolize love and passion, while blue might represent peace and trust. Different cultures may have different meanings for colours too. It's like a secret language spoken through colours!

COLOUR

COLOUR THEORY

COLOUR CHART

Exploring Colours in Science

Scientists also study how colours affect us. They explore how different colours can influence our thoughts, feelings, and even our decisions. It's a colourful world of discovery, where science meets the rainbow!

Screen Colours

Have you ever wondered how your tablet or phone displays so many colours? Screens use tiny lights called pixels, and each pixel can show millions of colours! These pixels combine red, green, and blue light in different ways to create all the colours you see on the screen.

The Magic of Colour Printing

Colour printing is like bringing a rainbow onto paper! Some printers use four colours – Cyan, Magenta, Yellow, and Black (CMYK) – to create a wide range of colours. When these colours mix together in different amounts, they can print almost any colour you can imagine.

Colours in Virtual Reality

Virtual Reality (VR) uses colours to create amazing, immersive worlds. When you put on VR goggles, you step into a world filled with vibrant colours and visuals. It's like jumping into a painting where everything around you is bursting with colour!

The Future of Colour Technology

Technology is always finding new ways to use colours. From super bright screens to realistic video games, colours help make our digital world more exciting and lifelike. Who knows what colourful inventions we'll see in the future!

Ancient Art and Natural Pigments

Long ago, artists made their own paints using natural ingredients. They used plants, minerals, and even insects to create a range of beautiful colours. This process was an art in itself, requiring skill and knowledge about nature's colourful resources.

Colours in Ancient Civilizations

Ancient civilizations, like the Egyptians, used colours not just for beauty but also for symbolism. They decorated their tombs and temples with colourful paintings using blue, red, gold, and more. Each colour had its own meaning and importance in their culture.

Famous Colourful Artworks

Throughout history, there have been many famous paintings known for their use of colour. Artists like Van Gogh and Monet used colours to express emotions and bring their visions to life. Their colourful masterpieces continue to inspire people all around the world.

Bioluminescent Colour in the Ocean

The ocean has its own magical colour light show called bioluminescence! Some sea creatures, like jellyfish and certain fish, can glow in the dark. This natural wonder creates a mesmerizing display of colours underwater, like a dance of lights in the deep sea.

Rare Colours in Animals

Some animals have incredibly unique and vibrant colours. From brightly coloured birds to iridescent insects, nature has a way of surprising us with its colour palette. These rare colours often have a purpose, like attracting mates or warning predators.

Beware! Very colourful birds!

The Northern Lights

One of nature's most spectacular displays is the Aurora Borealis, or Northern Lights. These lights create a magical dance of green, purple, and pink in the night sky. It's a rare and beautiful sight that reminds us of the wonders of our planet.

Unusual Colours in Plants

Even plants can surprise us with unusual colours. Imagine a meadow with rainbow-colored flowers, like blue roses or purple sunflowers. These rare and beautiful colours show the amazing diversity of nature's palette.

Reflecting on Our Colourful Journey

As we come to the end of our colourful journey, let's take a moment to reflect on all the amazing things we've learned about colours. From the deep blues of the ocean to the bright yellows of the sun, colours bring beauty and excitement to our world. They tell stories, evoke emotions, and connect us with nature.

www.ingramcontent.com/pod-product-compliance
Lightning Source LLC
Chambersburg PA
CBHW041539260326
41914CB00015B/1510